Contents

Introduction 5

A Brief History of the Panzerwaffe (1941-42) 6

The Tiger Tank Enters Service 8

Chapter One
Eastern Front and North Africa (1942-43) 11

Chapter Two
Sicily and Eastern Front (1943) 35

Chapter Three
Eastern and Western Front (1944) 69

Chapter Four
Last Year of War (1944-45) 97

Appendix I
Tiger Profiles 117

Appendix II
Tiger Tank Battalion History 119

Appendix III
Tiger Tank Battalion Markings 123

Appendix IV
Tiger Tank Battalion Equipment 124

Appendix V
Organisational Structure of Heavy Panzer 125

Appendix VI
Tiger Tank II Battalion (1944) 126

About the Author

Ian Baxter is a military historian who specialises in German twentieth-century military history. He has written more than fifty books including *Poland – The Eighteen Day Victory March*, *Panzers In North Africa*, *The Ardennes Offensive*, *The Western Campaign*, *The 12th SS Panzer-Division Hitlerjugend*, *The Waffen-SS on the Western Front*, *The Waffen-SS on the Eastern Front*, *The Red Army at Stalingrad*, *Elite German Forces of World War II*, *Armoured Warfare*, *German Tanks of War*, *Blitzkrieg*, *Panzer-Divisions at War*, *Hitler's Panzers*, *German Armoured Vehicles of World War Two*, *Last Two Years of the Waffen-SS at War*, *German Soldier Uniforms and Insignia*, *German Guns of the Third Reich*, *Defeat to Retreat: The Last Years of the German Army At War 1943–45*, *Operation Bagration – the Destruction of Army Group Centre*, *German Guns of the Third Reich*, *Rommel and the Afrika Korps*, *U-Boat War*, and most recently *The Sixth Army and the Road to Stalingrad*. He has written over a hundred articles including 'Last days of Hitler', 'Wolf's Lair', 'The Story of the V1 and V2 Rocket Programme', 'Secret Aircraft of World War Two', 'Rommel at Tobruk', 'Hitler's War With his Generals', 'Secret British Plans to Assassinate Hitler', 'The SS at Arnhem', 'Hitlerjugend', 'Battle of Caen 1944', 'Gebirgsjäger at War', 'Panzer Crews', 'Hitlerjugend Guerrillas', 'Last Battles in the East', 'The Battle of Berlin', and many more. He has also reviewed numerous military studies for publication, supplied thousands of photographs and important documents to various publishers and film production companies worldwide, and lectures to various schools, colleges and universities throughout the United Kingdom and the Republic of Ireland.

IMAGES OF WAR

HITLER'S HEAVY TIGER TANK BATTALIONS 1942-45

RARE PHOTOGRAPHS FROM WARTIME ARCHIVES

Ian Baxter

Pen & Sword
MILITARY

First published in Great Britain in 2020 and reprinted in 2023 by
PEN & SWORD MILITARY
An imprint of
Pen & Sword Books Ltd
47 Church Street
Barnsley
South Yorkshire
S70 2AS

Copyright of Ian Baxter, 2020, 2023

ISBN 978-1-52674-787-7

The right of Ian Baxter to be identified as author of this work has been asserted by him in accordance with the Copyright, Designs and Patents Act 1988.

A CIP catalogue record for this book is available from the British Library.

All rights reserved. No part of this book may be reproduced or transmitted in any form or by any means, electronic or mechanical including photocopying, recording or by any information storage and retrieval system, without permission from the Publisher in writing.

Typeset by Concept, Huddersfield, West Yorkshire HD4 5JL
Printed in the UK on paper from a sustainable source by CPI Group (UK) Ltd, Croydon, CR0 4YY

Pen & Sword Books Limited incorporates the imprints of Atlas, Archaeology, Aviation, Discovery, Family History, Fiction, History, Maritime, Military, Military Classics, Politics, Select, Transport, True Crime, Air World, Frontline Publishing, Leo Cooper, Remember When, Seaforth Publishing, The Praetorian Press, Wharncliffe Local History, Wharncliffe Transport, Wharncliffe True Crime and White Owl.

For a complete list of Pen & Sword titles please contact
PEN & SWORD BOOKS LIMITED
47 Church Street, Barnsley, South Yorkshire S70 2AS, England
E-mail: enquiries@pen-and-sword.co.uk
Website: www.pen-and-sword.co.uk

Introduction

Using rare and unpublished photographs, *Hitler's Heavy Tiger Tank Battalions* is an illustrated record of German heavy tank battalions or Schwere Panzer Abteilungen during operations on the Eastern, Western and Italian fronts between 1942 and 1945. It represents a visual account of the various elite battalion-sized tank units of the Wehrmacht and Waffen-SS equipped with the Tiger I and later Tiger II heavy tanks.

The book shows early formation units comprising twenty Tigers and sixteen medium Pz.Kpfw.IIIs, it illustrates the various vehicles that each battalion used in a supporting role, and the special independent Tiger tank maintenance companies which kept the vehicles in fighting condition. Much was owed by the Tiger tank battalions to their maintenance teams, which were able to quickly repair combat damage and return tanks to the battlefield to inflict more harm on the enemy.

The development of the Tiger tank battalions is traced from their deployment on the Eastern Front in 1942, Italy a year later, France in 1944, and to defensive actions outside Berlin in 1945. With detailed captions and text the book tells the story of how these battalions evolved and shows that although they were successful on the battlefield, mechanical unreliability continuously reduced the battalions to smaller and smaller combat-ready units. These heavy tanks, which were constantly required to fight offensive and defensive missions, were shuffled around and organised into ad hoc units according to conditions on the battlefield. Huge numbers were lost, but in spite of this the battalions fought on until the last days of the war, when the crews finally destroyed their equipment and surrendered to their enemies.

A Brief History of the Panzerwaffe (1941–42)

For the invasion of Russia, codenamed Barbarossa, the German army assembled some 3 million men, divided into 105 infantry divisions and 32 Panzer divisions. There were 3,332 tanks, over 7,000 artillery pieces, 60,000 motor vehicles and 625,000 horses. The Panzer divisions' heavy armour at that time comprised some 439 Pz.Kpfw.IVs, but for light armour it had to rely on obsolete light tanks.

For the Russian offensive the Panzer divisions had been slightly modified in armoured firepower and diluted in strength in order to form more divisions. The planners thought that by concentrating a number of Panzer divisions together they would be able to achieve massive local superiority.

These new Panzer divisions contained one tank regiment of two, sometimes three, Abteilungen, totalling some 150–200 tanks; two motorized rifle (schützen) regiments, each of two battalions, whose infantry were carried in armoured halftracks or similar vehicles, and a reconnaissance battalion of three companies (one motorcycle, two armoured cars). The motorized infantry divisions accompanying the Panzer divisions in the Panzergruppe were similarly organized, but badly lacked armoured support. The divisional artillery comprised of two field, one medium and one anti-tank regiment and an anti-aircraft battalion. These were all motorised and more than capable of keeping up with the fast-moving Panzers.

When the German invasion of Russian was finally unleashed on the morning of 22 June 1941 the Panzer divisions progressed exceptionally well and continued over the next several weeks penetrating deeply into Russia. By late July the German armies were fighting on a front more than 1,000 miles wide. The Panzer divisions had exploited the terrain and struck such a series of blows to the Red Army that commanders predicted that it was only a matter of time before the campaign would be over.

Inevitably the Panzer divisions were thinly spread out, and they were moving so fast that supporting units were barely able to keep pace with them. Nevertheless, between June and late September 1941, the panzer and motorized divisions were more or less unhindered by lack of supply. Neither did the terrain or weather conditions cause them problems. However, on 6 October the first snowfall of the approaching winter was reported. It melted quickly but turned the dirt roads to mud. Autumn had arrived. The Panzer divisions began to slow. Wheeled vehicles became stuck and had to be towed. The attack had been launched later than intended and preparations for bad weather were inadequate. There were no chains available for towing vehicles, no anti-freeze for engine coolant systems, and soldiers had no winter clothing.

In blizzards and temperatures which fell 30 degrees below zero, the Panzer divisions soon ran out of fuel and, within sight of Moscow, ran out of ammunition and were compelled to break off their attack. On 6 December plans to capture the Russian capital in 1941 had to be abandoned.

By 22 December only 405 tanks were operational in front of Moscow, 780 were out of action but repairable, 2,735 had been lost, and 847 replacements had arrived since 22 June. Less than 1,400 operational tanks remained. The heavy panzers had borne the brunt, and now the front was vulnerable to enemy tanks such as the new Russian T-34.

By the end of 1941 the battle-weary divisions of the Panzerwaffe were no longer fit to fight. Mobile operations had ground to a halt. Fortunately for the exhausted crews and supporting units no mobile operations had been planned for the winter of 1941, let alone for 1942. In the freezing temperatures most were pulled out of their stagnant defensive positions and transferred to France, to rest, reorganize and retrain.

In spite of the terrible problems that faced the depleted Panzer divisions, back in Germany production of tanks increased. To overcome the mammoth task of defeating the Red Army, more divisions were being raised, and motorized divisions were being converted into Panzergrenadier divisions. Although equipping the Panzerwaffe was a slow and expensive process, it was undertaken effectively with the introduction of a number of fresh new divisions being deployed on the front lines.

It was recognised by German High Command that it was not just the volume of tanks that was required; they needed heavier, stronger tanks too, to counter the Soviet T-34 medium and the KV-1 heavy tank, which were superior to anything the Panzerwaffe had available on the battlefield. Tank designers were busy discussing plans for the production of a heavy tank to be known as the Panzerkampfwagen VI Tiger Ausf. E, later shortened to Tiger I.

The Tiger Tank Enters Service

In April 1942 the German company Henschel & Son was given the task of producing the Tiger I on a large scale. The vehicle was the largest tank built in the Panzerwaffe, and was well gunned and armoured. Its frontal hull armour was 100mm thick. The frontal turret armour was 100mm with a 120mm thick gun mantlet. The hull side plates were 60mm thick, the side superstructures were 80mm, and the turret sides were 80mm.

Mounted on the Tiger was a deadly 8.8cm Kampfwagenkanone 36 (KwK 36), which had greater penetration power than the 7.5cm KwK 40 on the Sturmgeschütz III (StuG.III) and the Pz.Kpfw.IV.

The Tiger was powered by an upgraded HL230 P45 24-litre engine that developed 700 hp at 3,000 rpm. The tank's combat weight was a staggering 56 tons.

The internal layout was a standardised design typical of German tanks. It had a forward open crew compartment, with the driver and radio-operator seated at the front on either side of the gearbox. Three men were seated in the turret with the loader positioned to the right of the gun facing to the rear, the gunner to the left of the gun, and the commander behind him.

While the new Tiger was undoubtedly a great contribution to the war effort in Russia, production required considerable resources in terms of manpower and material, which was very expensive. In fact the Tiger I cost twice as much as the Pz.Kpfw.IV and four times that of the StuG.III.

Although from a technical point of view it was superior to anything else on the battlefield in 1942, when the vehicle came into service there was a shortage of qualified crews. They also required considerable amounts of fuel to run them, along with a large maintenance team to support them across Russia. A Tiger I required at least two standard German Sd.Kfz.9 Famo heavy recovery halftrack tractors to tow it, and because these recovery vehicles were in short supply it was often left to other Tiger tanks to recover broken down vehicles, which frequently resulted in over-heating and engines breaking down.

Despite these problems, the Tiger was a versatile machine. Due to its size and firepower its main purpose on the battlefield was for offensive breakthroughs. But by the time it became operational, the military situation on the Eastern Front and operations in North Africa had changed considerably. Instead of offensive actions its main use became defensive, being used primarily as a mobile anti-tank and infantry gun support weapon.

German tacticians decided on the formation of heavy tank battalions or Schwere Panzer Abteilungen. It was intended that the Tigers in these battalions would be able to fight on the offensive during breakthrough operations, and would be supported by either medium Pz.Kpfw.III or reconnaissance vehicles.

In 1942 a heavy tank battalion comprised twenty Tigers and sixteen Pz.Kpfw.IIIs, which in turn comprised two companies, each with four platoons of two Tigers and two Pz.Kpfw.IIIs. Each company commander would have an additional Tiger, and each battalion command would have another two.

These battalions would be deployed to critical sectors, either for breakthrough operations or, more typically, counter-attacks.

Supporting the Tiger tank apart from the Pz.Kpfw.III was a host of other vehicles which included the Sd.Kfz.7/1, Sd.Kfz.9, Sd.Kfz.10, Sd.Kz.251 halftrack and the Bergepanther armoured recovery vehicle. There were also numerous smaller vehicles such as the Sd.Kfz.2 Kettenkrad, motorcycles and motorcycle combinations, Kübelwagen, and support truck elements comprising infantry, Panzergrenadier, and maintenance teams.

The battalion was organised into a staff company consisting of a communications platoon of various armoured reconnaissance and communication vehicles, and engineer and anti-aircraft platoons. Each Panzer company consisted of three or four tanks, with medical service and repair vehicles in support. There was a workshop company consisting of two platoons with a recovery platoon, communications specialist, armourer, and spare part detachment.

Chapter One

Eastern Front and North Africa (1942–43)

As the Wehrmacht moved from one position to another in early 1942, Hitler examined his options after his first defeat of the war. He boldly revealed to his Generals that he would yet defeat the Russian Army, and announced that his forces would be refitted with the utmost speed. This included up-gunning the lighter panzers into anti-tank machines and modifying the StuG.III and Pz.Kpfw.IV.

As the German spring offensive, Operation Blau, was launched in southern Russia, Wehrmacht forces had stagnated around Leningrad, and the German central front had also ground to a halt sifting off its resources for the drive in the south.

Elsewhere, there was fighting in North Africa. Operating in the desert in 1941/42 the Deutsches Afrikakorps, or DAK, had made good use of its armoured vehicles under master-tactician General Erwin Rommel. His forces had smashed through British lines and by the end of June 1942 had broken through the Tobruk perimeter capturing some 35,000 prisoners. The British Eighth Army were forced to withdraw and victory for Rommel seemed certain. His force had taken a severe battering and by early July could only field forty-four tanks. Most of the transport vehicles had been captured or destroyed. In spite of this, the German push forward continued.

Meanwhile, on 23 July 1942, earlier than planned, Hitler ordered that the first Tiger tanks be transported to the Leningrad front. The first unit to receive the Tigers was the 1.Kompanie of Schwere Heeres Panzer Abteilung 502. Four Tigers accompanied by four Pz.Kpfw.III Ausf.N panzers were loaded onto special flatbed trains, chocked and sent to the Leningrad front. They arrived on 19/20 August and went into combat on the 29th. The terrain was swampy and forested and so their movement was restricted to roads and tracks. However there were few roads, and those that there were were boggy and the vehicles were pushed to their limits, which resulted in transmission problems and overheating engines. On the first day two of the Tigers broke down, but were recovered and repaired.

On 21 September, the Tigers, Pz.Kpfw.IIIs, and support and reconnaissance vehicles began operating as a unit. A few days later the rest of 1.Kompanie of the 502nd arrived at the front comprising of five Tigers and fourteen Pz.Kpfw.IIIs.

Further south, more Tiger tanks were dispatched to the front. This time to Schwere Panzerabteilung 503. This unit had been created on 4 May 1942 and was an independent battalion-sized unit equipped with the Tiger and Pz.Kpfw.III. The battalion was deployed in late 1942 to the Don front. By this period of the war the last throes of the battle of Stalingrad were being played out, and it was too late for it to participate in the relief operation, known as Winter Storm.

They arrived on 5/6 January 1943 and saw action on the 7th, participating in heavy defensive action in the Rostov-on-Don theatre. Fighting was fierce and again the Tiger developed mechanical problems with the transmission and overheating.

Back in North Africa, the tank corps were facing similar problems to those of the German army on the Eastern Front. Tons of supplies were shipped across the Mediterranean to reinforce the Axis forces in North Africa. Among the troops, artillery, flak and other weaponry were sixteen Pz.Kpfw.IIIs and three Tiger Is of the 501 Schwere Panzerabteilung 501, along with four Pz.Kpfw.IIIs that were organised with other units into Kampfgruppe Lueder.

Within a few weeks the strength of the 501 was eleven operational Tigers and sixteen Pz.Kpfw.IIIs. This was soon increased with another eight Tigers and eight Pz.Kpfw.IIIs which were assigned to the 756th Gebirgsjäger Infantry Regiment and Kampfgruppe Lueder, which was re-established with five Tigers and ten Pz.Kpfw.IIIs, and an additional battalion comprising the 1st Battalion of the 69th Mechanised Infantry Regiment.

The Tiger would be used extensively in prominent offensive and defensive operations in Tunisia. Although in small numbers, it was the most powerful tank in North Africa, and would become a revered machine among the Allies. By now Axis forces were undertaking a fighting withdrawal from Libya into Tunisia, and Rommel would owe much to the Tiger tank for its valued rearguard support.

The 21st Panzer Division saw extensive action trying to reach Tunis and was later supported by six Tigers and nine Pz.Kpfw.IIs from the 1st Company of the 501 which were attached to the 10th Panzer Division for Operation Frühlingswind.

On 14 February 1943 panzers managed to break through the Faïd Pass and became embroiled in heavy fighting at Sidi Bou Zid. It was here that Tigers knocked out twenty M4 Sherman tanks of the US 1st Armoured Division. On 26 February, the 501 was redesignated III/Panzer-Regiment 7 of 10 Panzer-Division. Each company received an additional fifteen Pz.Kpfw.IVs.

Despite the extra armoured support the Axis had sustained thousands of casualties in North Africa. Armoured vehicle losses were immense and replacements were too few to make up for them. Lack of fuel and spare parts, coupled with the need for trained crews, played their parts in weakenng the panzer units in Tunisia. Yet the Afrika Korps still continued to commit everything it had to the task in hand and called for more reinforcements.

As a result of Rommel's calls for help, a second unit, Schwere Heeres Panzer Abteilung 504, was transported to North Africa. It consisted of eighteen Tigers, twenty-five Pz.Kpfw.IIIs, and two Befehl-Tigers. The first three Tigers arrived in Tunisia on 12 March 1943, followed by another five over the coming weeks. The 1.Kompanie had eleven Tigers and nineteen Pz.Kpfw.IIIs, while the 2.Kompanie was held in Sicily with nine Tigers and six Pz.Kpfw.IIIs.

Nevertheless, the Panzergrenadier divisions were too exhausted to rectify the situation decisively. The Allies continued pushing forward while German forces were either forced to retreat or destroyed. Along the whole front the Afrika Korps were now reduced to skeletal formations on a stricken field. Now they were outnumbered and desperately short of fuel, lubricants and ammunition. As parts of the front caved in, armoured formations destroyed their equipment so that nothing was left for the conquering enemy. The Germans no longer had the resources to accomplish their objectives in Tunisia.

On 13 May 1943, the Axis forces in Tunisia finally surrendered, sealing the fate of the once seemingly invincible Afrika Korps. Any Tiger tank units that could be salvaged were immediately pulled out of the line and shipped to Sicily to help the deteriorating situation there.

An interesting propaganda photograph showing the well-known Tiger I named 'Tiki' of 8.Kompanie SS-Panzer Regiment 2 of the Das Reich Division on the Eastern Front.

(**Opposite, above**) An early production Tiger I in 1942. By April 1942 Henschel GmbH had been given the task of large-scale production of the Tiger I. There were numerous modifications made during the production run to improve automotive performance, firepower and protection. In 1942 alone, there were at least six revisions made, starting with the removal of the frontal armour shield. In May, mudguards were bolted onto the side of the pre-production run, and smoke candle dischargers were added on the turret sides in August 1942.

(**Opposite, below**) An early production Tiger I belonging to the Totenkopf Division. The Waffen-SS were allocated their own Tigers during the winter of 1942/3 and received a single heavy panzer company of fourteen Tigers.

(**Above**) An early production Tiger I has been loaded onto a special flat car and chocked in preparation for transportation to the Eastern Front in 1942. Rail was the quickest way to transport a heavy battalion to the front lines.

A rear view of an almost brand new standard early production Tiger tank. The turret has five spare track lines mounted on the turret side. The tank also has a full array of triple smoke candle dischargers on the turret as well as S-mine dischargers on the corners of the superstructure. It has a complete set of fenders as well as mud flaps. Note that the vehicle is covered in a base colour of dark yellow. It belongs to Schwere Panzer Abteilung 502.

(**Opposite, above**) A Tiger I belonging to Schwere Panzer Abteilung 503 during field trials. This battalion had been created on 4 May 1942 and was an independent battalion-sized unit equipped with the Tiger and Pz.Kpfw.IIIs. In late 1942 it was deployed to the Don Front in Russia.

(**Opposite, below**) An early production Tiger I belonging to Schwere Panzer Abteilung 502 seen undergoing maintenance on the Eastern Front in 1942. An engineer can be seen in the engine compartment. This vehicle belongs to the 3.Kompanie Schwere Panzer and features smoke candle dischargers on the turret and S-Mine dischargers on the edge of the hull roof at the front and rear corners. Note that the side fenders have been removed along with the folding segment of the rear mud flap.

(**Opposite, above**) A Tiger I halted near a village on the Eastern Front. Although difficult to see in the photograph, note the Tiger tank battalion marking on the front left of the tank painted in white which appears to be an elephant. The elephant was the mark of Schwere Panzer Abteilung 502.

(**Above**) A heavy prime mover wading along a typical Russian road following a downpour. The vehicle is towing a trailer, which would often be loaded with lighter vehicles that developed mechanical defects, and were being towed to a maintenance field workshop for repair.

(**Opposite, below**) A Waffen-SS Tiger awaiting transportation to the Eastern Front on a special railway flat car. One of the crew members can be seen perched on top of the vehicle.

(**Opposite, above**) A prime mover has halted in a field and is assisting a support vehicle which has become bogged down in marshy ground during operations on the Eastern Front. One of the crew members is attaching a cable to the halftrack to tow it out of the mud.

(**Opposite, below**) A column of Tigers on the advance along a road in Russia. Heavy Tiger tank battalions were used to threaten certain sectors of the front lines where they could often produce dramatic improvements in the local situation. Although its weight often made it difficult to move around areas which suffered from poor roads and weak bridges, the Tiger enjoyed a great advantage in firepower and survivability.

(**Above**) A battery of Sd.Kz.7/1 halftracks mounting the quadruple 2cm Flak 38. The weapons have been directed skyward and are more than likely being used to protect ground units.

Tiger during operations in Tunisia in early 1943.

Infantry can be seen hitching a lift on board an Sd.Kfz.10/4 halftrack which is manned by Luftwaffe personnel during operations on the Eastern Front in late 1942. Note that a number of infantry are sitting on the Sd.Ah.51 ammunition trailer.

A Tiger tank recovery vehicle can be seen with a chocked early production Tiger I secured on the trailer.

A winter camouflaged Mittlerer Zugkraftwagen 8-ton halftrack advances through a shallow river during operations in Russia in late 1942. These halftracks were used to tow ordnance to the battlefront but were also capable of serving as infantry transport. They were used in heavy Tiger tank battalions as a main support vehicle.

(**Opposite, above**) An Sd.Kfz.10/4 mounting a flak gun on the Eastern Front during winter operations in December 1942. These mounted flak guns were used in heavy Tiger tank battalions to support advancing armour against both ground and aerial attacks.

(**Opposite, below**) A Tiger from 13.Schwere Panzer Kompanie of Panzer Regiment 'Großdeutschland', which was formed from 3.Panzer Regiment 203 on 13 January 1943. They were originally equipped with nine Tigers and ten Pz.Kpfw.IIIs Ausf.L. 13.Kompanie fought at Kursk in July 1943.

(**Above**) A Tiger from Schwere Panzer abteilung 501 during operations in North Africa.

One of the new Tiger tanks sent to reinforce Axis forces in North Africa. Among the additional troops, artillery, flak and other weaponry there was a heavy Tiger tank battalion comprising sixteen Pz.Kpfw.IIIs and three Tiger Is of the 501st Heavy Panzer Battalion. These were the first elements of the battalion, along with four Pz.Kpfw.IIIs that were organised with other units into Kampfgruppe Lueder.

The crew of a Tiger I can be seen resting in the desert watching a Tunisian man with his camel passing by. This vehicle belongs to Schwere Panzer Abteilung 501. The tactical number 111 is painted in red with a white outline on the turret side.

Two photographs which are part of a series of images showing the initial deployment of the Tiger I to Tunisia in 1942. Both of these Tigers belong to the 1 Kompanie of Schwere Panzer Abteilung 501, represented by the large tactical sign 122 painted in red with a white outline. Of interest in the second photo are the crew's belongings attached to the turret bustle stowage bin and saplings applied to the vehicle for camouflage.

A series of four photographs showing a maintenance team changing the engine of an early production Tiger I during Abteilung 501 operations in Tunisia. The photograph shows a rotating 6-ton crane on a Bussing NAG 4500-Series 4.5 ton chassis either removing or installing the tank's Maybach HL210 P45 power plant. The final photo shows the maintenance crew taking a rest. Note the captured US Army Dodge WC-series truck parked next to the Tiger.

The crew of a Tiger I has halted near some vegetation during operations in Tunisia. This Tiger belongs to Schwere Panzer Abteilung 501. When it was shipped to North Africa at the end of December 1942 it was initially numbered 132. It was then renumbered 732 after the Beja Mission.

A Tiger from Abteilung 501 during operations in Tunisia in January 1943. These were formidable fighting machines whose arrival at the front was a welcome relief to the hard-pressed Afrika Korps. However, too few were delivered, and they were too thinly stretched to make any considerable dent against the growing tank might of the Allies.

A Tiger I rolls alongside a stationary staff car on a Tunisian road in January 1943. Note the canvas sheeting protecting the 8.8cm cannon's muzzle brake from dust and sand particles. This early production vehicle is also fitted with smoke candle dischargers which were mounted on the turret sides as a factory standard during this mid-war period.

Tiger tank 142 of 1 Kompanie Schwere Panzer Abteilung 501 on the advance in Tunisia. This tank was unloaded in Tunis and began operations in January. The first three Tigers of the 1.Kompanie were unloaded on 23 November in Bizerte in 1942 by the ship *Aspromante*. The remaining Tigers were shipped separately with the next one arriving on 27 November in Tunis. The remainder were shipped to Bizerte: two tigers on 1 December, one on 6 and 13 December, four on 25 December, five on 8 January, one on 16 January and the last two on 24 January 1943.

(**Above**) A column of Tiger I tanks of Abteilung 501 passes other stationary armour of the battalion on a desert road. Among the stationary vehicles appear to be an Sd.Kz.251 halftrack, a reconnaissance vehicle and another halftrack.

(**Opposite, above**) A Tiger tank has halted on a road and local Tunisians can be seen next to the vehicle. By early January 1943 the strength of Schwere Panzer Abteilung 501 was eleven operational Tigers.

(**Opposite, below**) A Tiger tank belonging to Abteilung 501 has halted on a road, and behind it a column of vehicles can be seen. The crew are sitting on the vehicle, a respite from the hot sweaty environment of their tank. Locals can be seen around the Tiger along with an Italian officer standing left of the tank.

A Tiger from Abteilung 501 rolls along a Tunisian road watched by an Afrika-Korps infantryman. The vehicle clearly shows the candle smoke dischargers attached to the turret sides.

A Tiger tank can be seen negotiating terrain during intensive operations in Tunisia in 1943. Over the coming weeks and months operational levels of the Tiger tank were reduced due to the overwhelming strength of the Allied forces. By mid-March, only eleven Tigers remained of Schwere Panzer Abteilung 501. These were then attached to Schwere Panzer Abteilung 504, which was the second Tiger unit to be sent to Tunisia. This heavy battalion was issued with twenty-five Pz.Kpfw.III and eighteen Tigers. It arrived in Tunisia with its battalion staff, workshop company, and 1 Panzer-Kompanie in Tunisia on 12 March 1943. The 2 Panzer-Kompanie remained in Sicily. The tank company had four platoons, each with two Tiger I tanks and two Pz.kpfw.III support tanks. By 12 May 1943 all of Schwere Panzer Abteilung 504 Tigers were destroyed or captured.

Chapter Two

Sicily and Eastern Front (1943)

On 10 July 1943 a combined Allied invasion of Sicily began with amphibious and airborne landings in the Gulf of Gela. Land forces comprised the US Seventh Army and the British Eighth Army. The intended plan was for a drive by the British northwards along the east coast to Messina, with the Americans in a supporting role along their left flank.

Sicily was defended by about 200,000 Italian, 32,000 German and 30,000 Luftwaffe ground troops. The main German formations were the Panzer Division Herman Göring and the 15th Panzergrenadier Division. The Panzer Division had 99 tanks in two battalions, but was short of infantry, while the 15th Panzergrenadier Division had three grenadier regiments and a tank battalion with sixty tanks.

Attached to Panzer Division Herman Göring were seventeen Tigers under the 2.Kompanie of Schwere Heeres Panzer Abteilung 504. When the Americans arrived in their landing zone on 11 July they were met by heavy attacks from the 504. Fighting was vicious and in three days ten of the seventeen Tigers were destroyed. To prevent complete destruction, 504 withdrew and sent the last Tigers back across the Straits of Messina to Italy.

The departure of the 504 meant Axis forces making a full-scale withdrawal from the island, but in spite of the overwhelming strength of the Allies, the evacuation proved highly successful.

Meanwhile on the Eastern Front, the situation had become stabilized. Although many parts of the Russian Front had stagnated, in the south German forces were making steady progress. Kharkov had been recaptured in March 1943, and the central front was steadily building up reserves.

This German success brought renewed confidence to German High Command, and prompted Hitler to plan for a major offensive in the centre and south. Already the Panzerwaffe had been building up strength and by early summer fielded some twenty-four divisions on the Eastern Front. This was a staggering transformation. Hitler now intended to risk his precious Panzerwaffe in what became the largest tank battle of the war, known as Operation Citadel, around the city of Kursk.

To support 'Zitadelle' there would be a host of new up-gunned and up-armoured panzers and panzerjägers (tank hunters). By June, twenty-one Panzer divisions, including four Waffen-SS divisions and two Panzergrenadier divisions, were being prepared for Zitadelle in the Kursk salient. By early July there were seventeen divisions and two brigades with no less than 1,715 Panzers and 147 Sturmgeschütz III (StuG) assault guns. Each division averaged some ninety-eight Panzers and self-propelled anti-tank guns. At this time the new Pz.Kpfw.V 'Panther' Ausf.A, despite production problems, made its debut.

Supporting the main armoured punch through Kursk, and what would become the backbone of the Panzerwaffe during the offensive, was the Tiger tank. For this battle Schwere Heeres Panzer Abteilung 505 was deployed for action. This was the last independent Tiger tank battalion, formed in February 1943, comprising several Tigers and twenty-five Pz.Kpfw.IIIs. The 505 was deployed in Army Group Centre in April and upgraded for the offensive to eleven Tigers.

Despite the Panzerwaffe's impressive array of firepower for Kursk, there was still an acute shortage of infantry, which was to lead to panzer units taking on more ambitious tasks normally reserved for soldiers. To make matters worse, by the time the final date had been set for the attack as 4 July, the Red Army knew the German plans and had made their preparations. For three months there had been extensive building and various other preparations to counter the German attack. Russian commanders knew exactly the strategic focal point of the German attack. The Panzerwaffe were determined to use their tried and tested Blitzkrieg tactics, but the immense preparations that had gone into constructing the Soviet defences meant that this was never going to succeed.

When the attack was finally put into motion before dawn on 5 July 1943, the Germans were stunned by the dogged defence of the Soviet forces. The two heavy Tiger tank battalions (503rd and 505th), with one battalion each on the northern (505th) and southern (503rd) flanks, found the enemy defensive positions far stronger than first predicted. Yet, in spite of the resistance, the 503rd and 505th only lost four Tigers each during the Kursk offensive. The 503rd had a full complement of forty-five Tigers for Kursk which included twenty-four brand new Tigers that it had received in April of that year.

Apart from the two heavy Tiger tank battalions at Kursk the 13.Kompanie/Panzer Regiment Grossdeutschland, which was formed from Panzer Regiment Grossdeutschland in January 1943, also received fifteen operational Tigers, and none of these Tigers were lost in the battle.

Other Tigers to see action in the offensive were to be found in the Waffen-SS, notably the 1.SS-Panzer Korps. At the start of the battle thirty-five of them were made operational.

However, as the battle progressed losses mounted and eventually the Wehrmacht were forced to take their first painful steps of retreat back to the German frontier. The Russians had managed to destroy no less than thirty divisions, seven of which were panzer. German reinforcements were insufficient to replace the staggering losses, so they fought on under-strength until Hitler pulled them out of the line to avoid complete annihilation. The German forces at Kursk had borne the brunt of the heaviest Soviet drive. The Russian Voronezh and Steppe fronts had possessed massive local superiority against everything the Germans could field.

July to December 1943 saw the Tiger tank battalions grow in size. Over the next five months the 503rd, 505th, 506th, 507th, 508th and 509th heavy Tiger tank battalions all received additional Tigers on the Eastern Front. The 503rd received twelve replacement Tigers in August, the 505th had its first five shipped on 23 September, the 506th became the first independent battalion to be created with an original complement of forty-five Tigers which it received in August, the 507th, which was formed on 23 September 1943, was also equipped with Tigers but did not have a full complement of forty-five until late December/early 1944. The 508th was another battalion to receive forty-five Tigers in late December but was withdrawn and ordered to Italy to defend Anzio. The 509th was another new Tiger tank battalion formed in September and this also received a full complement of forty-five Tigers. The battalion began arriving on the Eastern Front on 28 October.

Supporting the battalions were the independent units such as Schwere Panzer Kompanie (FKL) 316 which was issued with ten Tigers in September. The III Abteilung/Panzer Regiment Großdeutschland also boasted an entire heavy tank battalion of three companies with forty-five Tigers, which was created for the Panzergrenadier Großdeutschland. Its first company of Tigers was provided by the old 13.Kompanie which had fought at Kursk. By the end of August the battalion was at the front embroiled in heavy fighting in the Ukraine.

On 19 July I.SS-Panzer Korps, which had seen action at Kursk, received a heavy Tiger tank battalion, Schwere SS-Panzer Abteilung 101. This comprised two new heavy companies created from 13.Kompanie of the SS-Panzer Regiment 1. However, this heavy battalion was pulled out of Russia in response to the Allied landings in Sicily.

Another heavy Tiger tank battalion also made its debut in the second half of 1943, Schwere SS-Panzer Abteilung 102. This was created in October and each of the heavy tank battalions would be attached to a Corps of the Waffen-SS. Originally, each heavy tank battalion was composed of a single company of Tiger Is, attached to each respective SS Panzer Division in the Panzerkorps.

The last heavy tank battalion that operated in the Waffen-SS and was created in July was Schwere SS-Panzer Abteilung 103. This did not see action properly on the Eastern front until the following year with parts of its battalion sent to Yugoslavia to fight as infantry in later 1943.

(**Opposite, above**) A Tiger I halted on a road during operations in Italy. Two crew members can be seen standing next to their machine. The tank has track links attached to the turret sides for additional protection.

(**Opposite, below**) A Tiger from Schwere Panzer Abteilung 504 rolling through a Sicilian town during defensive operations in 1943. The battalion was attached to the Panzer Division Herman Göring and comprised seventeen Tigers under the 2.Kompanie. When the Americans arrived in their landing zone on 11 July they met with heavy attacks from the 504. Over the course of three days ten of the seventeen Tigers were destroyed.

(**Above**) On a road during defensive operations in Italy are three Pz.Kpfw.IV Ausf.Gs with a stationary support vehicle. Pz.Kpfw.IVs, especially during the latter part of the war, were often found in Tiger battalions or ad hoc units fighting in a supporting role.

(**Opposite, above**) Two stationary Tiger tanks can be seen with German infantry during operations in Italy. Track links are bolted to the turret sides. One vehicle has received an application of tropical camouflage. As in North Africa, during the Italian campaign many vehicles were given sand colour schemes, almost identical to those used in the Afrika Korps. In Italy the terrain could be very similar, and for that reason the vehicles were completed in the tropical colours of yellow brown RAL 8000, grey green RAL 7008, or brown RAL 8017.

(**Above**) A column of Tigers advance along a road during a withdrawal operation. To prevent complete destruction, Schwere Panzer Abteilung 504 was ordered to withdraw and its units were sent across the Straits of Messina to Italy.

(**Opposite, below**) Tiger tanks have been loaded on board special flatbed trains destined for the front lines. Some 1,350 Tiger Is were manufactured during the war. They only ever served in dedicated heavy tank detachments that were deployed at corps or army level.

(**Opposite, above**) A knocked-out Tiger from Schwere Panzer Abteilung 504 during the Sicilian campaign in July 1943. This battalion was equipped with seventeen Tiger Is and was assigned to Panzer-Division 'Herman Göring' on 9 July. Ten Tigers were lost during the first three days of fighting and over the following weeks the unit was pushed back towards Messina where during the nights of 10 and 11 August the remaining armoured vehicles and one Tiger were ferried across to mainland Italy.

(**Opposite, below**) A Tiger I belonging to Abteilung 508. This Tiger was modified with a rig cable of placing charges. This was to increase the local defence of the tank. The Tiger was photographed near Anzio bridgehead and more than likely had been knocked out of action.

(**Above**) Many of the Axis nations were keen to obtain Tiger tanks. In this photograph a Japanese officer inspects a Tiger I. Note the Zimmerit anti-magnetic mine paste on the armoured sides.

This photograph was taken at the Henschel Works in Kassel in July 1943 and shows a Tiger being put through its paces in a demonstration for two Japanese officers.

An interesting set of five photographs showing the Panzer ace General Heinz Guderian inspecting a Tiger I in 1943, accompanied by Waffen-SS officers. These Tiger Is are early versions with the drum cupola. The insignia of the 'Leibstandarte' Schwere SS-Panzer Abteilung 101 can be seen on the front left of the Tiger in one of the photos.

A Tiger I belonging to Abteilung 503 during field exercises in 1943. The battalion saw extensive combat in Army Group Don in early 1943 and served with a number of divisions of the 4th Panzer Army where it was tasked with securing the withdrawal of Army Group A. The unit took part in March 1943 in the third battle for Kharkov and then received a full complement of forty-five Tigers in May in preparation for the Kursk offensive.

Panzergrenadiers dressed in their familiar Waffen-SS camouflaged smocks support Tiger tanks of the 'Das Reich' division during the initial stages of the Kursk offensive in July 1943.

A photograph showing late production Tiger Is belonging to III Abteilung, Panzerregiment 'Großdeutschland'. These vehicles have been loaded onto SSYMS railroad flatbed cars. The photo contains a gantry crane in its folded retracted travel position. This crane was essential for the removal of the Tiger's turret for maintenance and also so that the transmission drive unit could be lifted out through the turret ring.

A Tiger halted in a field next to a group of Waffen-SS infantry in a slit trench overlooking a position. Note the national flag draped on the turret of the tank for aerial recognition.

Pz.Kpfw.IVs and a Pz.Kpfw.III are on the advance with other armoured vehicles including motorcycles in July 1943.

A Tiger during operations at Kursk in July 1943. For the offensive two heavy Tiger tank battalions (503rd and 505th) were deployed for action. The 503rd had a full complement of forty-five Tigers for Kursk including twenty-four brand new Tigers that it had received in April of that year. Supporting the attack was the 13.Kompanie/Panzer Regiment 'Großdeutschland' which received fifteen operational Tigers for the battle; none of these Tigers were lost.

A Tiger tank belonging to Schwere Panzer Abteilung 503 during operations in July 1943. This early production vehicle clearly shows the candle smoke dischargers attached to the turret sides. Its tactical number 211 is painted in red with a white outline.

A Tiger during the start of the Kursk offensive advancing through the maze of intricate defensive enemy positions.

(**Above**) A Waffen-SS Tiger tank with supporting SS grenadiers in a field during the Kursk offensive in July 1943. Despite the Germans' impressive array of firepower for Kursk, there was still an acute shortage of infantry which was to lead to panzer units, notably the Tiger, taking on more ambitious tasks normally the preserve of soldiers.

(**Right**) Two maintenance men can be seen using a steel wrench to remove a Tiger's tracks to repair its wheels. This Tiger belongs to Abteilung 503.

(**Opposite, above**) Three late production Pz.Kpfw.III Ausf.Ms negotiating a typical muddy Russian road following a downpour in the summer of 1943. These tanks were equipped with the long 5cm gun, 20mm hull and turret side skirts, and the deep-wading exhaust pipe system for river crossings.

(**Opposite, below**) Showing the 2cm FlaK 38 quadruple mount in action. This gun could produce a hurricane of fire, being able to discharge 1,800 rounds per minute from its four barrels. It had two operators: one fired the top left and bottom right guns, the other fired the top right and bottom left guns. The loader could quickly change the magazines while the other continued to fire.

A Russian peasant can be seen next to an early production Tiger tank which is appears to be undergoing some maintenance while using the house as cover.

This photograph of a halted Tiger gives an excellent view of the port-hole containing the MG34 machine gun, and the slit visor for the driver.

Two photographs taken in sequence depicting Tiger tanks that were to be transferred to Schwere Panzer Abteilung 502 during a training exercise in France. This heavy battalion was formed during the summer of 1942 and was the first unit to see action on the Eastern Front around Leningrad in August 1942. It went on to see further action in Russia and saw engagements through 1943 around Lake Ladoga and the Newel area near Belarus. It later covered retreating German forces from the Leningrad area in late 1943.

(**Opposite, above**) Another vehicle used in Tiger tank battalions was the versatile amphibious four-wheel-drive off-roader known as the Schwimmwagen. In this photograph Waffen-SS soldiers can be seen driving it, armed with a mounted MG42 machine gun.

(**Opposite, below**) A Tiger I belonging to the Schwere Panzer Abteilung 503 in a field during a fire mission against enemy targets in 1943.

(**Above**) Two crew members can be seen sitting on the roof of a Pz.Kpfw.IV during its transportation by flat-bed railcar to the front.

Two Pz.Kpfw.IIIs Ausf.M on the advance through a Russian village. It was intended that for the Tigers to be able to fight on the offensive during breakthrough operations they would be supported by either medium Pz.Kpfw.III or reconnaissance vehicles.

This image depicts the major modifications needed to keep the old Pz.Kpfw.IV in combat service for so long. This Ausf.H variant has hull side plates and turret sides protecting it. The Pz.Kpfw.IV saw extensive service in the heavy Tiger tank battalions throughout the war and became a major reason for the Tiger's longevity.

An interesting photograph showing a mid-production Tiger I with the new improved cast commander's cupola. The vehicle has clearly been knocked out of action and belonged to Schwere Panzer Abteilung 509. Note the passing Russian horse-drawn 76.2mm Infantry Gun Model 1927.

A maintenance crew are repairing a damaged track on a Tiger I, possibly from Schwere Panzer Abteilung 502 on the Eastern Front. Note some of the road wheels have been removed and the hull of the Tiger blocked up with wood beams to replace them. Note the Fieseler Storch nearby, which has dropped in to see how repairs are progressing.

The crew of a Tiger I pose for the camera standing next to their tank during a halt in their march in 1943. Note the vegetation attached to the side of the vehicle for camouflage.

The crew of a Pz.Kpfw.III Ausf.M have halted in a field during operations on the Eastern Front. This variant was fitted with spaced armoured skirts or Schürzen: armour plating installed around the turret and on the hull sides.

A photograph taken at the rear of a Tiger I during operations at Kursk. This tank belonged to one of the three Waffen-SS heavy tank companies. Note the spare track links and the crew's helmets and water bottles slung around the turret sides. The national flag has been draped over the turret roof for aerial recognition.

During operations in 1943 and the flak crew can be seen with their 2cm Flakvierling 38 quadruple self-propelled flak gun. The gun is mounted on the back of an Sd.Kfz.10/4, which was widely used with a variety of flak guns. These weapons often supported heavy Tiger tank battalions from potential ground and aerial attacks.

Tiger tank belonging to Abteilung 503 negotiates a ridge during operations in 1943. Some officers and other ranks can be identified in the field watching the manoeuvres.

A maintenance crew are seen repairing a Tiger I. Note that some of the road wheels have been removed and the hull of the Tiger blocked up with wood beams to replace them.

Two excellent photographs showing a Tiger tank and crew belonging to Schwere Panzer Abteilung 505 in Orsha. Note the Tiger tank battalion marking of a knight on a horse stencilled in black on the turret side indicating it belongs to the 505.

A crewmember poses for the camera standing on top of his Tiger during a lull in the action in 1943. This vehicle belongs to Schwere Panzer Abteilung 502, which participated extensively in various engagements on the Eastern Front during 1943 and 1944.

A Tiger tank can be seen passing a burnt-out building. The vehicle has its muzzle brake protected by canvas sheeting indicating the tank is not battle-ready.

Pz.Kpfw.IV and Tiger crews have a group photograph during a lull in fighting on the Eastern Front. All are wearing their distinctive black panzer uniforms.

An interesting and rare chance to see a Tiger tank belonging to Schwere Panzer Kompanie SS Panzer-Regiment 2 'Das Reich' during a halt in their march on the Eastern Front. The vehicle is sitting exposed in a field with its barrel at the six o'clock position.

(**Opposite, above**) A mid-production Tiger during winter operations on the Eastern Front. The vehicle has received an application of winter camouflage paint. Note the ditching log attached to the tank and cable used to change tracks, which are both stored on the superstructure side plate.

(**Opposite, below**) A Tiger I rolls along a Russian road during the late winter of 1943. For a Tiger tank a hard frost was much easier going than rain or thaw. Even after the failed Kursk offensive, winter operations that year still saw heavy Tiger tank battalions demonstrating their awesome killing power on the battlefield. Between late July and December 1943 the 503rd, 505th, 506th, 507th, 508th and 509th heavy tank battalions all received additional Tiger tanks to support their efforts on the Eastern Front.

(**Above**) A close-up view of a mid-production Tiger I on the Eastern Front in late 1943. Note the Zimmerit anti-magnetic paste over the vehicle and barbed wire attached to the armoured sides to discourage infantry attackers.

In a snowy field in late 1943 on the Eastern Front is a Pz.Kpfw.III command vehicle operating, complete with antennae. In the distance a battery of what appears to be a column of *Wespen* are on the advance. The *Wespe* by late 1943 had become a popular vehicle; it was armed with a 10.5cm leFH 18/2 L/28 gun and protected by a lightly armoured superstructure mounted on the chassis of a Pz.Kpfw.II. They served in numerous armoured artillery battalions, but because of their light armour many were lost in battle.

Tiger tank crews wearing reversible jackets white side out converse during winter operations in late 1943. A Tiger I with a complete application of whitewash camouflage paint stands on a road.

Chapter Three

Eastern and Western Front (1944)

Through January and February 1944 on the Eastern Front, the winter did nothing to impede the Soviet offensives from grinding further west. Army Groups A and South still held about half the ground between the Dnieper and Bug rivers, but in a number of areas the front was buckling under the strain of repeated Soviet attacks. Army Group South was being slowly pressed westwards, its Panzers unable to strike a decisive counter-blow because of the Führer-order to stand fast on unsuitable positions. Consequently, Panzerwaffe units found themselves tied down trying in vain to hold back the Soviet drive. These battles became known as the 'cauldron battles' or Kesselschlachten.

By April mud finally brought an end to the almost continuous fighting in the south and there was respite for the Panzerwaffe in most areas of the front. Despite the setbacks, there grew a renewed feeling of motivation in the ranks of the Panzerwaffe. Confidence was further bolstered by the efforts of the armaments industry as more Tiger tanks came off the production lines, 301 Tigers entering service, 80 per cent of which were operational by the early summer of 1944. During this period ninety-eight Tigers were distributed among the SS-101, SS-102 and the (FKL) 316, which would soon be committed to the Normandy sector in northern France. The 504th and 508th had seventy-eight Tigers available, and these were preparing to transport to defensive action in Italy. The 503rd, following a rest and refit, saw operational duties in Russia with a full complement of forty-five Tigers between February and March 1944, before being withdrawn to Normandy.

On the Eastern Front, the 505th, 506th, 507th, 509th, 510th and the famous Panzerregiment Großdeutschland were used to support the crumbling front lines. Originally the Tiger's intended role had been as a breakthrough weapon, but now as the situation had deteriorated, its main use was defensive, as a mobile anti-tank and infantry gun support weapon. Also they were stretched along a very thin Eastern Front, and as a result Tiger tank battalions mostly fought actions in which they were not at full strength. Tiger battalions were often ordered to prop up parts of the front with hastily constructed battle groups drawn from a motley collection of armoured formations well below strength. Great demands put upon the heavy Tiger tank battalions during the spring and summer of 1944. Constant and unpredictable action, coupled with the nightmare of not having enough supplies, perpetually beset the minds of the Tiger commanders. The Red Army, encouraged by the Germans dire situation, was mounting bolder and bolder operations.

On the Western Front the military situation soon mirrored that of the Eastern. In Northern France in June 1944 there were three Schwere Panzer Abteilungen equipped with Tiger I tanks that saw operations including a small number of Tiger Is with the Panzer Lehr Division. The 503rd was transferred to Normandy with thirty-three Tiger Is and twelve of the new Tiger II, or 'King Tiger B' as it was then referred to, reaching the battlefield in early July 1944. The King Tiger B was undoubtedly a formidable fighting machine whose arrival at the front was a welcome relief to the hard-pressed Panzerwaffe. Nonetheless the situation was not good. The Schwere SS-Panzer Abteilung 101 arrived in Normandy in June and by the end of the month the 1st Kompanie had lost fifteen of its forty-five Tigers. It was pulled out in July to refit with the new Tiger II.

Alongside 101 was Schwere SS-Panzer Abteilung 102, transferred to Normandy with a full complement of 45 Tiger Is, reaching action in early July following a shipment delay. Fighting in France was fierce and by 20 July the battalion reported it still had forty-two Tigers of which seventeen were operational. By the end of the month it had thirty operational, but by early September all had been lost. What was left of the unit was ordered to return to the training grounds for a rest and refit with the Tiger II.

Another battalion supporting the defence was Schwere Heeres Panzer Abteilung 503. This battalion had been withdrawn from combat in late April for a rest and refit and then transferred back to the west where it received thirty-three Tiger Is and twelve Tiger IIs. It saw action on 11 July, and during its furious withdrawal through France where it bitterly contested large areas of ground, it lost most of its armour in August 1944. On 9 September it was once again pulled out of the front and ordered to rest and refit with the Tiger II.

On the Eastern Front the position was grimmer still for the German war machine. While the Panzerwaffe fought for survival in France, in Russia the Red Army opened up a new offensive on 22 June, the third anniversary of the Soviet invasion, launched against Army Group Centre, known as Operation Bagration. The three German armies opposing them had thirty-seven divisions, weakly supported by armour, against 166 divisions supported by 2,700 tanks and 1,300 assault guns. At the end of the first week the three German armies had lost between them nearly 200,000 men and 900 tanks; 9th Army and the 3rd Panzer Army were almost annihilated. The remnants of the shattered armies trudged back west to try to rest and refit what was left of its Panzer units and build new defensive lines. But any plans to regain the initiative on the Eastern Front were doomed forever.

As for the heavy Tiger tank battalions that were embroiled in the Russian Bagration offensive, they too had been severely mauled. Schwere Heeres Panzer Abteilung 501 and the 505 played key roles in defensive operations. The 505th was placed in the 5th Panzer Division. This division was sent direct from the Ukraine by rail to help block the advancing Russian forces on the Moscow–Minsk highway. It was reinforced with some Pz.Kpfw.IIIs, 55 Pz.Kpfw.IVs, 70 Panthers, and 29 Tiger Is belonging to the 505th. The main objective of the 505th was to hold the Berezina river line and allow withdrawing units of the Fourth Army to retreat to safety. When the 5th Panzer Division arrived there was utter confusion in the area. Littered along the roads going west over the Berezina bridges there were countless burning vehicles and abandoned equipment. Troops were demoralised, exhausted and often without weapons. Stocks of supplies were almost non-existent and many soldiers had not eaten in days.

During the withdrawal operation, to keep the main railways lines open for evacuation to the north of Minsk the 5th Panzer Division concentrated its main armour consisting of Schwere Heeres Panzer Abteilung 505 and Panzer 31st Regiment. The 505th bore the brunt of many of the attacks, but scored well against the advancing Russian armour. In just six days of combat it had knocked out no less than 295 Soviet tanks of which 128 were destroyed by Tiger tanks.

Over the next few days the division's formidable tank strength was reduced from its original seventy Panthers, fifty-five Pz.Kpfw.IVs and twenty Tigers of the 505th, to just twelve Panthers, six Pz.Kpfw.IVs and two or three Tigers. Luckily for the tank crews a number of the knocked-out Panzers could be successfully salvaged from the battlefield by one of the independent maintenance companies and taken to a nearby workshop to be repaired to fight another day.

As for the 505th, it was all but destroyed, and its remnants pulled out of the front and sent back to Germany to be refitted with the Tiger II.

Desperation gripped the battered and bruised front lines and troops were now becoming more than ever reliant on the Tigers and Panthers for defence. Since 1942 the Tiger had dominated the battlefield on the Eastern Front, and although in 1944 there were never enough available for the defensive battles, they still played a key role. Again and again these armoured monsters demonstrated their awesome killing power playing a prominent roles alongside their heavy battalions against numerically superior Soviet armoured forces. But with the tide turned against the German army they were overstretched and being slowly destroyed, and there were hardly any replacements.

Panzergrenadiers supported by a whitewashed Tiger I during a mission in the snow.

Tigers often were compelled to support infantry attacks due to the lack of weapons and consequently many were lost. In this photograph a Tiger I can be seen advancing in support of Panzergrenadiers during winter operations in Russia.

During winter operations on the Eastern Front a Tiger I can be seen on the move. The vehicle has a full application of winter whitewash camouflage and Zimmerit anti-magnetic mine paste applied. Barbed wire has also been attached to the side to fend off enemy infantry.

Out in the snow and Tiger tanks are being replenished with ammunition. The crew can clearly be seen transferring rounds for the KwK36 L/56 main gun into the Tiger tank.

(**Opposite, above**) Panzergrenadiers clad in their winter whites take up position in the snow while two Tiger tanks can be seen moving in their familiar sweeping formation across the arctic wasteland of Russia.

(**Above**) An Sd.kfz.10/4 halftrack mounting the familiar quadruple flak gun pointing skyward. By 1944 air attacks against German armoured columns became so severe that heavy Tiger tank units were often compelled to move only at night.

(**Opposite, below**) A column of Tiger Is bound for the front can be seen rolling along an icy road. By early 1944 the Panzerwaffe were being pressed westwards.

(**Above & right**) Two photographs showing a halted Kübelwagen on a muddy road. These staff, utility, reconnaissance cars were to be found in heavy Tiger tank battalions.

(**Opposite**) Two photographs taken in Vinnitsa on the Eastern Front in early 1944 showing Tigers belonging to the I SS Panzer Korps. This heavy Waffen-SS battalion was created on 19 July 1943 as a part of the I SS Panzer Korps, by forming two new heavy tank companies consisting of Tiger I tanks and incorporating the 13th (Heavy) Company of the 1st SS Panzer Regiment. It was attached to 1st SS Panzer Division Leibstandarte. In late 1943 the 1st and 2nd company of the battalion was sent to Russia while the remainder stayed in the west.

A number of Sd.Kfz.251 halftrack personnel carriers and late variant Pz.Kpfw.IVs can be seen during operations on the Eastern Front in the winter of 1944. The halftrack, especially the Sd.Kfz.251, was a versatile vehicle which could travel across some of the most rugged terrain. While these halftracks were primarily used to transport infantry personnel to the forward edge of the battlefield they were often tasked for reconnaissance missions because of their speed and useful firepower.

Clad in their winter whites the crew of a 3.7cm FlaK36 mounted on an Sd.Kfz.6/2 are preparing a defensive position during winter operations on the Eastern Front. These flak guns were used against both ground and aerial targets and were found in some Tiger tank battalions.

Four photographs showing the Sd.Kfz.2, or what the Germans called the Kleines Kettenkraftrad HK 101 or Kettenkrad. Initially this vehicle was a motorcycle tractor for airborne units or Fallschirmjäger, but later served in Heeres and Panzerwaffe units, notably heavy Tiger tank battalions. There were two variants of the vehicle, Sd.Kfz.2/1 and Sd.Kfz.2/2. Both were used with a trailer and had field communication gear mounted behind the driver. It was primarily tasked with laying communication cable from a special mounted wire spool. However, it was versatile and could be used for a variety of other tasks such as pulling heavy loads and carrying troops. Later in the war the Kettenkrads also appeared in reconnaissance patrols and independent scout detachments, and were used especially where roads were almost impassable due to mud or dense forests.

(**Above**) A number of support vehicles halted in the snow with a stationary motorcyclist. During the early part of the war, a great number of motorcyclists rode into battle and dismounted to fight. However, it soon became apparent that they were very vulnerable to small arms fire and booby traps, and some units began relegating them from front line duties to communication and reconnaissance duties, at which they excelled, especially in the heavy Tiger tank battalions.

A Tiger I belonging to Schwere Panzer Abteilung 507 near Tarnopol after the relief operation in mid-April 1944. The infantry on the march through the city are more than likely elements of the 9th SS Panzer-Division 'Hohenstauffen' and a number of ad hoc units assembled together.

Crossing a shallow river is a column of vehicles including an Sd.Kfz.251 halftrack and a support truck.

Five photographs showing an independent Tiger tank battalion maintenance team undertaking repairs to a Tiger. Much was owed to the specialist maintenance companies that kept these tanks in fighting condition. The photographs show the large portal crane which was used to remove the heavy turret, or the engine, for repairs.

After removing the turret, the mechanics were able to place it on wooden blocks or a purpose-built wooden horse.

A platoon of Tiger Is advancing across a field in formation towards the front. This was a typical tactical advance by the independent Tiger tank battalions going into action. Sweeping the front in formation was the most effective way of defeating an enemy.

Two photographs showing a late variant Pz.Kpfw.IV during operations in Russia in the early summer of 1944. For additional reinforcements it became common practice for Tiger tank battalions to receive Pz.Kpfw.IVs.

An interesting photograph showing a late model Tiger I from Schwere Panzer Abteilung 506 in a spot of trouble. It appears that the wooden bridge has collapsed under the weight of the Tiger and the tank has become stuck.

In early May 1944 in Kolomea, Hungarian tank crewmen are being trained to operate the Pz.Kpfw.IV, StuG.III and Tiger I. The Tiger belongs to Schwere Panzer Abteilung 503. After crew training the unit handed over ten tanks to the Hungarian army.

A Tiger I belonging to Schwere Panzer Abteilung 503 has expertly concealed itself between a tree and a house. Note the national flag draped near the cupola for aerial recognition.

A tank crew of Abteilung 503 converse next to their Tiger during operations in Normandy in July 1944. The 503 was an independent battalion-sized unit assigned to a single corps. The s.Pz.Abt.503 saw extensive fighting in Normandy and by August was almost destroyed during Operation Goodwood.

Tiger 323 from the 3./s.SS Panzer Abteilung 101 makes its way to the front in Normandy on 7 June 1944, with SS-Hauptscharführer Barkhausen in the commander's cupola.

Tiger 221 from SS Panzer Abteilung 101 can be seen negotiating a road in northern France. The Leibstandarte (LSSAH) SS Panzer Corps had been re-formed in early July 1944 to incorporate the 12th SS Panzer-Division 'Hitlerjugend'. The LSSAH had been in a holding position north of the River Seine before the Normandy invasion to counter a possible landing in the Pas de Calais area; the first units did not arrive in the Normandy sector until the night of 27/28 June, with the whole division taking another week to arrive.

A Volkswagen Kübelwagen is stationary on the side of the road with troops conversing. On the road support vehicles are burning, more than likely attacked by enemy aircraft. In northern France the Germans found movement by road during the day perilous as columns of vehicles were exposed to constant air attacks. This led to units moving mainly at night or through woods.

A Tiger tank rolling along a road in Normandy. Despite the reversal on the western and eastern fronts, these vehicles continued to represent a formidable foe.

An abandoned Tiger I inside a French town in the summer of 1944. American soldiers can be seen looking at the vehicle along with members of the French resistance.

A well camouflaged Sd.Kfz.10/5 has halted on a road during the campaign in France in the summer of 1944. It mounts the 2cm Flak 38. Passing the vehicle is a Sd.Kz.251 halftrack personnel carrier.

Two photographs showing knocked-out Tiger tanks in the Falaise Pocket. The Battle of the Falaise Pocket ended the Battle of Normandy with a decisive German defeat with more than forty German divisions destroyed. Hundreds of German tanks and armoured vehicles were lost at Falaise, with surviving units retreating through France over the Seine to avoid complete annihilation.

Two photographs taken in sequence showing Pz.Kpfw.IVs operating in a field and a German infantry defensive position during the Russian summer offensive, Operation Bagration. It was Schwere Panzer Abteilungen 501 and 505 that played key roles in the defence operations. The 505th was placed in the 5th Panzer Division and sent direct from the Ukraine by rail to help block the advancing Russian forces on the Moscow–Minsk highway. It was reinforced with a number of Pz.Kpfw.IIIs, fifty-five Pz.Kpfw.IVs, seventy Panthers, and twenty-nine Tiger Is.

(**Opposite, above**) A late model Tiger I fitted with steel wheels during operations in Lithuania in late August 1944. The troops hitching a lift are men of the 21st Luftwaffe Field Division. This Tiger belongs to Schwere Panzer Abteilung 510 which was formed in mid-1944 and saw extensive action in the Baltic States and East Prussia.

(**Opposite, below**) On the Eastern Front in the summer of 1944 is a late production Tiger I belonging to Schwere Panzer Abteilung 507. Note the logs to the side of the tank.

(**Above**) During operations in Russia the crew of a Tiger I prepares to camouflage their vehicle with foliage to conceal it from aerial and ground surveillance. This tank belongs to Schwere Panzer Abteilung 506. This battalion saw action at Lemburg, Tarna and Krivoi-Rog in the Ukraine until the summer of 1944. Due to severe losses it was withdrawn from battle and sent to Germany in August 1944 where it was refitted with Tiger IIs.

Tigers from Schwere Panzer Abteilung 509 advancing through a forested area in late 1944. This battalion was in Army Group Centre from the summer of 1944 and following the Russian Bagration offensive its units were pushed back into Poland where the battalion lost sixteen Tigers near Kielce. In December the battalion was attached to IV SS Panzer Corps which was preparing to relieve the encircled garrison of Budapest.

Chapter Four

Last Year of War (1944–45)

By June 1944 the German army was fighting a war on three fronts: France, Russia and Italy. In Italy in August the Allies had advanced beyond Rome, captured Florence, and were closing in on the Gothic Line, which was the last major defensive line between Pisa and the Apennines between Florence and Bologna to the Adriatic coast.

To reinforce the defensive lines across Italy there were a number heavy Tiger tank battalions supporting the Panzerwaffe. The 504th had been completely rebuilt with a full complement of 45 Tigers in March. It was originally earmarked for the Eastern Front, but due to Allied success in Italy the battalion was transferred to Italy in early June 1944. Soon it was embroiled in action trying, in vain, to stem the Allied drive north. Within weeks the battalion lost half its Tigers, and with only twelve replacements it fought on, being supported by a number of Pz.Kpfw.IVs, anti-tank guns, tank-destroyers and assault guns such as the Hetzer, Jagdpanther and Jagdtiger. In fact tank-destroyers and assault guns outnumbered the tanks, which was confirmation of the Panzerwaffe in its defensive role.

Another heavy Tiger tank battalion to see extensive defensive action in Italy was the 508th. In January 1944 it had been ordered to take up a defensive disposition around Anzio, and was later outfitted with Panthers and Ferdinands. In May and June it received twenty-seven replacement Tigers and saw action in August around Pisa. In early September 1 Kompanie moved across to Savignano in eastern Italy; on the drive eleven Tigers were lost to mechanical problems. The 2 Kompanie reported it had no tanks left and was ordered to pull out of line and was sent back to Paderborn in Germany. As for the 3 Kompanie, it advanced from Bologna and moved via Imola, Faenza, and Forli to Cesena, where it was put into line to oppose the northward drive of British forces on the Adriatic Front.

By 1 October only fifteen tigers were operational: ten in 1st Kompanie, two in the 2nd, three in the 3rd. Later in the month, the Allies pushed German lines up to northern Italy, but the 508th fought on. First Kompanie saw some success during defensive fighting in Faenza and south of Solarolo, but through January and early

February 1945 the tanks were mostly used in a defensive artillery role. Then, with losses mounting the battalion gave its last remaining Tigers to the 504th and returned to Germany to be fitted out with the Tiger II.

Meanwhile on the Western Front the Allies had advanced through France and now threatened Holland and Belgium. The British planned on a combined air and land attack to liberate the Dutch cities of Eindhoven, Nijmegen and Arnhem, and then advance into Germany. However, unbeknown to the Allies, there were two powerful Panzer divisions recuperating, 9th SS Panzer Division 'Hohenstaufen' and 10th SS Panzer Division 'Frundsberg', behind the lines.

When the Allied assault was finally launched on 17 September 1944, Operation Market Garden, they were immediately met by strong German resistance and soon ran into difficulty. There followed a series of heavy battles in the city of Arnhem. Both sides became exhausted, but it was the Germans who received the first major reinforcements. Schwere Panzer Abteilung 506, which comprised of a number of Tiger tanks, was quickly moved in as a blocking unit to support units of the Frundsberg division. German armour however turned out to be inferior to the British, and the assault units were ordered to withdraw on the night of 25/26 September. British units had been battered nonetheless, and the depleted forces withdrew across the Lower Rhine at Oosterbeek and retreated south.

The battle of Arnhem was a military failure for the Allies. Although the Germans had been severely weakened by months of fighting in France, the blow they had inflicted on their foe in Holland was greater.

For the next several weeks German forces on the Western Front continued to recuperate and refit with additional armour and troops scraped from Eastern Front. For some time German planners had been gathering their troops for what was to be Germany's final attempt to regain the military initiative in the west, a bold offensive in Belgium codenamed *Wacht am Rhein* (Watch on the Rhein).

A large number of divisions were assigned to the Ardennes, including heavy Tiger tank battalions. For the attack ninety Tiger IIs were mobilised with Schwere SS Panzer Abteilung 501 which was attached to the 1SS Panzer-Division. The lead section of the 501 was commanded by the veteran armour ace Obersturmbannführer Joachim Peiper. Schwere Panzer Abteilung 506 had forty-seven Tiger IIs and was attached to the 6th Panzer Army and reinforced by Schwere Panzer Abteilung 301 in the 9th Panzer Division. Main armoured vehicles used in the 1SS Panzer-Division included the Pz.Kpfw.IV Ausf.H, Pz.Kpfw.V Ausf.G Panthers, Pz.Kpfw.VI Tigers, Pz.Kpfw.VI Ausf.B King Tigers, Bison Ausf.M Sd.Kfz.138/1 150mm sIG 33/2 howitzer carrier (rear mounted) and Wirbelwinds.

The 653 and 654 Panzerjäger battalions also saw action in the Ardennes and were equipped with the Panzerjäger Tiger Ausf. B. The composition of this heavy battalion comprised a battalion of halftracks, plus a Wirbelwind battery, a supply company, 2

Kompanie (614 Jagdpanzer Kompanie) with three platoons of Jagdpanzer VI (Elefants), while the 3 Kompanie had three platoons of four Jagdtiger each.

In the first twenty-four hours of the offensive the Germans used every means at their disposal to annihilate all enemy resistance. But the Allies soon recovered from the initial surprise. Resistance stiffened day by day and by late December the Americans began stemming the German drive. Lack of fuel and constant congestions on the narrow roads brought many German units to a standstill. The fuel shortages were so bad that on 23 December Peiper's Kampfgruppe destroyed their vehicles, and his remaining 1,000 men set out on foot for the German lines.

By mid-January 1945 the 506th had lost forty-four of its twenty-seven Tiger IIs, and by 17 January they had to destroy fourteen Tiger IIs and one Tiger I that could not be repaired.

On the Eastern Front, great efforts were being made to hold onto Hungary and to relieve Budapest. Elsewhere the Panzerwaffe continued to commit everything to the fight against the Soviets, but they possessed too many tanks, anti-tank guns and aircraft for the panzers which remained incapable of causing any serious losses or delay to the advance. The Russians continued pushing forward while German forces retreated through Poland to East Prussia. Along the Baltic coast too Soviet forces advanced crushing all that remained of the once mighty Army Group North.

In early 1945 few reinforcements were reaching the front lines, and understrength Panzer divisions were combined ad hoc to form new units with a handful of tanks and Panzergrenadiers. Among these ad hoc units were the Pz.Abt.500 'Paderborn', named after the training grounds from which its vehicles had come; it had seventeen Tigers and was put into line in Russia on 21 October 1944. At the end of January 1945 the 'Ersatz Brigade' Großdeutschland fought with two Tigers. On 23 February 1945, Panzer Abteilung 'Kummersdorf' received the last 5 Tiger Is and joined an ad hoc unit known as Panzer Division 'Müncheberg'. Apart from its Tigers, 'Kummersdorf' possessed two Pz.Kpfw.IVs, one Pz.Kpfw.III, one Nashorn, two captured M4 Shermans, four Sd.Kfz.233 and 231 other vehicles including one Elefant, Jagdtigers, and an Italian P-40 tank, and a number of Sd.Kfz.251 halftracks.

(**Above**) Seen here is a column of later model Pz.Kpfw.IVs with intact Schürzen inside a town during operations in Italy in-mid 1944.

(**Opposite, above**) A Tiger I has lost its track. To reinforce the defensive lines across Italy there were several heavy Tiger tank battalions supporting the Panzerwaffe. One was Schwere Panzer Abteilung 504 which had been completely rebuilt with a full complement of forty-five Tigers in March 1944.

(**Opposite, below**) A Tiger I with infantry hitching a lift advancing along a road bound for the front. By August 1944 the Allies had advanced beyond Rome, captured Florence, and were closing in on the Gothic Line, the last major defensive line between Pisa, the Apennines, Bologna and the Adriatic coast.

Movement through Italy was often hard for the Tiger tank battalions and resistance strong. In this photograph a crew from Schwere Panzer Abteilung 508 are preparing to fit a track onto their vehicle concealed in the undergrowth. The shells have been removed for safety and ease.

A Tiger has halted on the main road to Rome. This tank belongs to Schwere Panzer Abteilung 508. On 1 August 1944 only fourteen Tigers were operational out of the twenty-eight available in the battalion. The 508th reached the vicinity of Pisa on 14 August.

Two photographs showing a maintenance crew repairing the damaged track of a Tiger during operations in Italy in 1944. Up to late 1944 maintenance companies were able to recover and repair up to a staggering 75 per cent of tanks damaged in combat or broken down due to defect or mechanical problems. Most damage to tanks was by anti-tank rifles or mines to the tracks or drive wheels. Tigers often had large power jacks as part of their standard equipment which made it possible to repair tracks in the field. Lost drive wheels or return rollers were a bigger issue.

(**Above**) Two photographs showing Tigers from Schwere Panzer Abteilung 508 driving through Rome in May 1944. The battalion was equipped with Pz.Kpfw.IIIs and fought a vicious withdrawal through Rome while being attached to various German infantry units. After Rome fell on 4 June, the battalion began a general withdrawal north, and was used to prevent the Germany army in Italy being cut off. During the withdrawal thirteen Tigers were destroyed and abandoned by their crews because of mechanical failures. When the battalion reached Poggibonsi it was equipped with new Tigers, bringing its combat strength to thirty-seven. It fought in Italy until the end of the war.

(**Opposite, above**) An abandoned Tiger can be seen among some olive trees in Italy in 1944. The vehicle has a full application of Zimmerit anti-magnetic mine paste. Track links have also been bolted onto the turret sides for additional armoured protection.

(**Opposite, below**) Fallschirmjäger troops hitch a lift aboard a Tiger tank as German forces withdraw through a forest during the Ardennes offensive on the Western Front. By this time production of the Tiger I had been terminated in favour of the superior Tiger II or 'King Tiger'. However, numbers of the new machines were simply not enough to avert the catastrophes unfolding on both fronts.

(**Opposite, above**) During the initial stages of the Ardennes offensive and a Tiger II rolls along a road followed by two motorcyclists armed with the MP40 machine pistol. Moving in the opposite direction is a column of American troops captured during the initial stages of the Ardennes offensive.

(**Opposite, below**) An interesting photograph showing a 3.7cm flak gun mounted on a vehicle overlooking a road. By this period of the war Tiger tanks were being hastily thrown together into various ad hoc units named after their commanders. They consisted of a motley assortment of weapons and armoured vehicles.

(**Above**) Panzergrenadiers on the march supported by a halftrack. Panzergrenadiers were frequently seen in the thick of battle moving alongside armoured vehicles and providing the latter with valuable support.

Parked in a field this Panzerwerfer is being prepared for a fire mission. This version was designated as the Sd.Kfz.4/1 and consisted of an armoured Maultier body with a ten-shot fifteen Nebelwerfer 42 rocket launcher mounted on the roof. This vehicle was known by the Germans as the Maultier or 'Mule' and was often seen supporting heavy tank battalions during the latter part of the war.

Various armoured vehicles including two Pz.Kpfw.IVs and halftracks supporting an advance through a wooded area in Belgium in late 1944. Halftracks were the best way of getting to the battlefield, or away from it.

Two photographs taken in the Hungarian capital Budapest showing Tiger IIs from Schwere Panzer Abteilung 503. By mid-December German forces had been pushed back to Budapest with this battalion fighting to relieve the city in Operation Konrad. On 4 January 1945 Schwere Panzer Abteilung 503 was renamed Schwere Panzer Abteilung 'Feldherrnhalle', after its commander. In spite of fighting with distinction against superior Russian forces the relief operation of the capital failed and the battalion withdrew.

(**Above**) A Tiger I from Schwere Panzer-Kompanie 'Hummel' near Geilenkirchen on 16 October 1944. This unit was formed on 20 September 1944 by Schwere Panzer Ersatz und Ausbildungs Abteilung 500 and was transported west equipped with fourteen Tigers for defensive actions in Holland. On 8 December 1944 the battalion was renamed Schwere Panzer Abteilung 506.

(**Opposite**) A Schwimmwagen Type 166 amphibious car of a Tiger tank battalion staff travelling through a forest. The metal commander pennant for a Panzer division commander can be seen on the right mud guard.

(**right**) Infantry hitching a lift aboard a halftrack during operations on the Eastern Front in early 1945.

The crew of a Tiger II can be seen with their tank during a halt in their advance during winter operations on the Eastern front in early 1945. This Tiger belongs to Schwere Panzer Abteilung 509. The battalion fought hard in Hungary, and on 18 January 1945 was embroiled in Operation Konrad III where it was tasked with the relief of Budapest. During the operation the 509th lost forty of its forty-five Tiger IIs, with ten being total losses. Remnants of the battalion were then transferred to III Korps to support Operation Frühlingserwachen in March 1945. From there it retreated to Vienna where it fought a defensive action.

A crew pose for the camera standing next to their Tiger II during a pause in defensive actions in early spring 1945. They belong to Schwere Panzer Abteilung 503.

Two photographs showing captured Tiger IIs abandoned on the Eastern Front in 1945. Due to mechanical breakdowns and lack of fuel, crews often abandoned the tanks, sometimes not even having time to destroy them.

An interesting photograph showing a captured Panzerjäger Tiger Ausf.B in a field in 1945. This monster mounted a 12.8cm PaK 44 L/55 gun on Tiger II chassis and could out-range and defeat any Allied or Soviet tank. Although 150 of these vehicles were ordered for front-line duties only around eighty were produced. They were too heavy and suffered mechanical problems and did nothing to change the course of the war.

What appears to be a Polish soldier examining a knocked-out Tiger I in 1945. It has clearly been hit at the side, as twisted skirting is evident from the shell's impact.

Two photographs of the same captured Jagdtiger. One shows the vehicle on a Gotha 80-tonne trailer being prepared to be taken to England for inspection. Although the firepower of the Jagdtiger was lethal, its mobility was restricted mainly due to fuel shortages and mechanical breakdowns. They were also very slow moving and a relatively easy target for Allied fighter-bombers.

A knocked-out Tiger I near Berlin in April 1945. This tank probably belonged to Abteilung 503 which fought in the area.

Appendix I

Tiger Profiles

Panzerkampfwagen VI Tiger Ausf.E

This Tiger is from Großdeutschland Panzergrenadier Division which was attached to the 2nd SS Das Reich Division and has a camouflage scheme of dark sand base RAL 7028 with stripes of olive green RAL 6003 and brown RAL 6003. The Tiger I was regarded as the backbone of the Panzerwaffe. It was well built and well armed, but it was expensive and labour-intensive to build. It also had track problems, a short range and high fuel consumption. In spite of this, the vehicle was generally mechanically reliable, powerful, and successful against Soviet armour. The Tiger I had impressive frontal hull and turret armour 100mm thick and a 120mm-thick gun mantlet making it very difficult to knock out for either anti-tank artillery or tank rounds. It was armed with a 56-calibre-long 8.8cm KwK 36. *(Tom Cooper)*

Panzerkampfwagen Tiger Ausf.B (Königstiger)

This Tiger is from Stab Schwere Panzer-Abteilung 501 and is shown during the defence of Berlin in April 1945. It has a camouflage scheme of dark sand base RAL 7028 with broken stripes of olive green RAL 6003. The Tiger II was the successor to the Tiger I, combining the latter's thick armour with the armour sloping used on the Panther medium tank. It weighed almost 70 tons and was protected

by 100–185mm of armour to the front. It was armed with the long barrelled 8.8cm KwK 43 L/71 anti-tank cannon. It was issued to heavy tank battalions of both the regular army and the Waffen-SS and was first used in combat with Schwere Panzer Abteilung 503 for defensive actions in Normandy in July 1944. *(Tom Cooper)*

Appendix II

Tiger Tank Battalion History

Schwere Panzer Abteilung 501
Formed in the summer of 1942, it was transported to Tunisia in December 1942. The battalion saw action at Hamra, Tebourba, and Kasserine in February 1943. It surrendered in May 1943 after defensive action in the Medjerda Valley. It reformed in France and then its full complement shipped to the Eastern Front in November 1943 where it fought in Vitebsk and Gorodok. It was destroyed during Operation Bagration in July 1944. Nevertheless, it was reformed with Tiger IIs, and was transported to the Eastern Front where it was redesignated 424 Battalion. It then undertook fierce defensive action and withdrew through Poland and saw fighting in the Ardennes and then Hungary. Equipped with Tiger IIs, in March 1945 it had a reported strength of thirty-two tanks of which eight were operational. On 19 March Heinrich Kling was appointed commander and the unit was known as Kampfgruppe Kling until the end of the war.

Schwere Panzer Abteilung 502
This heavy battalion was formed during the Summer 1942 and was the first unit to see action on the Eastern Front around Leningrad in August 1942. However, due to the unfavourable terrain several of its Tigers developed mechanical problems or became stuck in the mud, and a number were captured by Russian units due to lack of supporting armour and infantry. During Operation Bagration in summer 1944, the battalion retreated into the Kurland 'cauldron' and fought a defensive action around Memel and Königsberg. It was then transported west where it saw action in Normandy in July 1944. The battalion then rested and was refitted with Tiger IIs. On 5 January 1945 it was redesignated 511 and took part in the defence of the Oder Front. During the Battle of Berlin in April 1945 it was encircled in the Halbe Pocket, and in May it surrendered to Russian forces.

Schwere Panzer Abteilung 503
Formed in the spring of 1942, the battalion was transported to Russia in January 1943 where it spearheaded the German winter counter-offensive. In July 1943 it fought at Kursk, and then was compelled to withdraw to the Dnieper as part of III Panzer-Korps. In January 1944 it became part of a Panther battalion and formed what was

known as 'Heavy Panzer Regiment Bäke'. With Bäke the battalion saw extensive action in battles around Cherkassy. In April 1944 it was pulled out of the line and went west where it rested and was refitted with Tiger IIs. Two months later it saw intense fighting in Normandy where it suffered heavy losses to naval gun fire and fighter-bombers. The battalion was again pulled out of battle and fully refitted in September 1944, where it was despatched to Hungary. It was renamed Schwere Panzer Abteilung 'Feldherrnhalle' and attached to the Panzergrenadier Division of that name. The entire division fought fiercely in Operation Konrad, the failed attempt to relieve Budapest in January 1945, and was later destroyed during the last weeks of the war on the Eastern Front.

Schwere Panzer Abteilung 504

Created in January 1943, the bulk of this battalion was shipped to Tunisia where it saw extensive fighting around Maknassy and Medjerda. The remainder of the battalion was transported to Sicily, but withdrew to the Italian mainland after resisting the Allied Sicily landings. It then was withdrawn, rested and fitted in Holland where it was sent back to Italy to undertake defensive actions around Anzio as part of Hermann Göring Panzergrenadier Division. The battalion saw extensive fighting and was moved along the Gothic Line where it became heavily embroiled in defensive action. The 504 stayed in Italy until it surrendered in May 1945.

Schwere Panzer Abteilung 505

This battalion was created in January 1943, and sent to the Eastern Front where it was attached to the 9th Army in Army Group Centre. It first saw fighting during the Kursk offensive in July 1944, and led the main spearhead of the northern front of the Kursk Salient. It remained in the region as Army Group Centre stagnated. However, when the Red Army launched their Bagration offensive in June 1944, it was almost wiped out. Late that summer it was withdrawn, rested, and refitted with Tiger IIs. It was then sent back to the Eastern Front where it fought in defensive battles initially against the Narev bridgeheads in the Baltic states and in East Prussia supporting the 24th and 25th Panzer Divisions. The unit continued fighting until the end of the war.

Schwere Panzer Abteilung 506

This battalion was formed in July 1943, and saw heavy defensive battles along the Dnieper as part of Army Group South. It saw action at Lemburg, Tarna and Krivoi-Rog in the Ukraine until the summer of 1944. Due to heavy losses it was withdrawn from battle and sent to Germany in August 1944 where it rested, and was refitted with Tiger IIs. The battalion was called upon to assist German armoured units during enemy airborne operations in Holland in September 1944. Two months later it was assigned to I SS Panzer Korps where it saw heavy fighting in the Ardennes offensive in

December 1944. It was then moved to fight in Hungary and then withdrawn for the defence of the 'Homeland' where it saw extensive defensive action in the Ruhr region. It finally surrendered to American units in the Ruhr pocket in April 1945.

Schwere Panzer Abteilung 507

This battalion was created in September 1943, where it was sent to Russia in the defence of Tarnpol, Vitebsk and the Narev River until January 1944. At this time the 507 was the only battalion that was overstrength: it had fifty-five Tigers. But after two weeks of the Russian winter offensive of mid-January 1945 only seven Tigers remained. On 6 February it was pulled out and ordered to Germany to refit with Tiger IIs. It served in Germany until February 1945, and then went to Czechoslovakia where it lost all its Tigers. It never returned.

Schwere Panzer Abteilung 508

Formed in August 1943 the battalion was shipped to Italy in January 1944. Here the unit spearheaded the German offensive against the Allied bridgehead at Anzio and became enmeshed at Nettuno where it suffered heavy losses as it withdrew through Italy. In early 1945 it gave its last fifteen Tigers to the 504th and was transported back to Germany to be refitted with Tiger IIs. It was then transported to the Western Front. The unit was disbanded in February 1945 following heavy losses.

Schwere Panzer Abteilung 509

This battalion was formed in September 1943, and saw action in Russia in the regions of Kirovograd, Zhitomir and Kiev. The unit was temporarily attached to the 2 SS Panzer Division 'Das Reich' in late 1943 and fought at Kamenetz-Podolsk. The following year it saw extensive defensive action in the Soviet counter-offensive in the southern sector of the front in 1944. Later that year it returned to Germany where it was rested and refitted with Tiger IIs. In January 1945 it was sent to Hungary as part of IV SS Panzer Korps. Following heavy fighting it withdrew and surrendered to American forces in Austria after losing all its tanks in action.

Schwere Panzer Abteilung 510

Created in June 1944, the battalion was sent to Russia to fight against the Red Army's 'Bagration' summer offensive. In East Prussia, the battalion was divided into two sections, one supporting the 30th Infantry Division, the other supporting the 14th Panzer Division. Both sections saw heavy fighting in the Kurland Peninsula in early 1945. In March, two companies were withdrawn to Kassel in Germany, leaving behind thirteen Tigers fighting with the 14th. The battalion surrendered with its fifteen Tiger Is to the Red Army in Kurland. The 510 was the only Tiger battalion never to have been equipped with Tiger IIs; it remained fighting with late-variant Tiger Is.

Schwere Panzer Abteilung 512
This battalion was created for Jagdtiger Tank Destroyers.

Schwere Panzer Abteilung 301
Formed in the summer of 1944, this unit was equipped with Tiger Is and BIV remote-controlled demolition robot armoured vehicles. It was dispatched to the Western Front in November 1944 and saw heavy fighting in the Ardennes Offensive, where it was destroyed.

Schwere Panzer Abteilung 'Kummersdorf'
This battalion was formed in February 1945 purely for defensive action in the battle of Berlin. It saw heavy fighting with the 'Müncheberg' Panzer Division in April and but was soon destroyed.

101 SS Schwere Panzer Abteilung
Formed from the Leibstandarte's Tiger company in the autumn of 1943 as the heavy battalion assigned to the newly formed I SS Panzer-Korps, this Waffen-SS battalion was transported to Normandy in June 1944 to undertake defensive action. The celebrated commander Michael Wittmann fought with the unit until he was killed in action near Caen. The battalion was later re-equipped with Tiger IIs, and saw fighting in the Ardennes and then Hungary. It was re-designated 501 in early 1945.

102 SS Schwere Panzer Abteilung
This battalion was formed to support II SS Panzer Korps. It was sent to fight in Normandy from June 1944. Later that year it was re-equipped with Tiger IIs. It was re-designated 502 in early 1945.

103 SS Schwere Panzer Abteilung
Formed in 1943 with Tiger Is, this battalion saw no action until it was re-equipped with Tiger IIs and then sent to Russia to undertake defensive action there.

Appendix III

Tiger Tank Battalion Markings

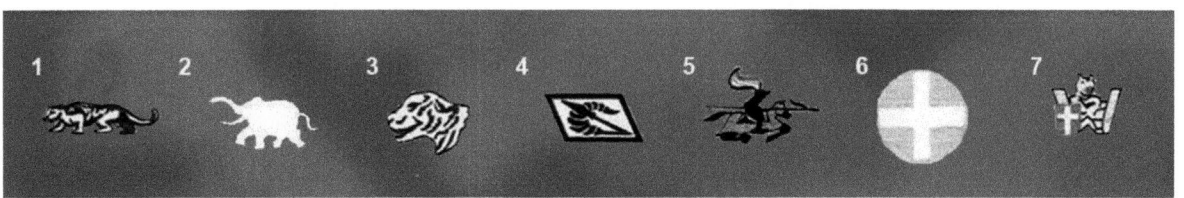

1. sPz.Abt.501;
2. sPz.Abt.502;
3. sPz.Abt.503;
4. sPz.Abt.504;
5. sPz.Abt.505;
6. sPz.Abt.506 [1944];
7. sPz.Abt.506 [1943–1944];
8. sPz.Abt.507;
9. sPz.Abt.508;
10. sPz.Abt.509.

Appendix IV

Tiger Tank Battalion Equipment

Description	Vehicle type
Flakpanzer IV	Self-propelled anti-aircraft gun
Sd.Kfz.7/1 8-ton 4 × 2cm Flak	Self-propelled anti-aircraft gun
Sd.Kfz.251 Schützenpanzerwagen	Armoured halftrack
Bergepanther	Armoured recovery vehicle
Sd.Kfz.9 18-ton Zugkraftwagen	Halftrack prime mover
Sd.Kfz.10 1-ton Zugkraftwagen	Light halftrack
Sd.Kfz.2 Kettenkrad	Gun tractor
Beiwagenkrad	Motorcycle with sidecar, e.g. BMW R75
Solokrad	Motorcycle
Kübelwagen Personenkraftwagen	Staff car
Personenkraftwagen, zivil	Civilian car
Lastkraftwagen	Truck, e.g. Opel Blitz
Lastkraftwagen, zivil	Civilian truck
Maultier	Halftrack
Kran-Kraftfahrzeug	Mobile crane

Appendix V

Organisation Structure of Heavy Panzer Battalion

Staff company
 Three tanks
 Communications platoon
 Armoured reconnaissance platoon
 Area reconnaissance platoon
 Engineer platoon
 Anti-aircraft platoon

Three Panzer companies (fourteen tanks each)
 Company detachment (two tanks)
 Three Panzer platoons (four tanks each)
 Medical service
 Vehicle repair detachment
 Two combat trains
 Baggage train

Workshop company
 1st and 2nd workshop platoon
 Recovery platoon
 Armourer detachment
 Communications detachment
 Spare part detachment

Appendix VI

Tiger Tank II Battalion (1944)

Battalion Command	3 × Tiger II
1–3 Company Command	2 × Command Tiger II
1 Platoon	4 × Tiger II
2 Platoon	4 × Tiger II
3 Platoon	4 × Tiger II

Notes

Notes